The Madonna Painter

The Madonna Painter

or

The Birth of a Painting

MICHEL MARC BOUCHARD

TRANSLATED BY LINDA GABORIAU

TALONBOOKS

Talonbooks
P.O. Box 2076, Vancouver, British Columbia, Canada V6B 3S3
www.talonbooks.com

Typeset in New Baskerville and printed and bound in Canada.

First Printing: 2010

The publisher gratefully acknowledges the financial support of the Canada Council for
the Arts; the Government of Canada through the Book Publishing Industry Develop-
ment Program; and the Province of British Columbia through the British Columbia
Arts Council and the Book Publishing Tax Credit for our publishing activities.

Le Peintre des madones was originally published in French in 2004 by Leméac Éditeur,
and in Italian translation (*El pintor de madonas o El nacimiento de un cuadro*) in 2003
by Ubulibri.

For more information on the author, please consult: www.michelmarcbouchard.com.

Rights to produce *The Madonna Painter*, in whole or in part, in any medium by any
group, amateur or professional, are retained by the author. Interested persons are
requested to contact his agent: John C. Goodwin & Associates, 839 Sherbrooke est,
Suite 2, Montréal, Québec H2L 1K6; tel.: (514) 598-5252; www.agencegoodwin.com.

LIBRARY AND ARCHIVES CANADA CATALOGUING IN PUBLICATION

Bouchard, Michel Marc, 1958–
[Peintre des madones, ou, La naissance d'un tableau. English]
        The madonna painter, or, The birth of a painter / Michel
Marc Bouchard ; translated by Linda Gaboriau.

Play.
Translation of: Le peintre des madones, ou, La naissance
        d'un tableau.
ISBN 978-0-88922-641-8

        I. Gaboriau, Linda II. Title. III. Title: Birth of
a painter. III. Title: Peintre des madones, ou, La naissance
d'un tableau. English.

PS8553.O7745P4413 2010   C842'.54   C2010-900439-6

… for Louis Gravel
who was part of the adventure from the beginning.

Man created the gods, the opposite has yet to be proven.
— SERGE GAINSBOURG

AUTHOR'S NOTE

The action takes place in a village that has the same name as my native village, but the language of the play is not that of its inhabitants. My characters simply echo the medieval beliefs that shaped their destiny until recently. They inspired this story, with their gossip about the marital spats between God and Satan.

It was in Florence, the city of a thousand Madonnas, that I wrote down this fable, loosely inspired by the events surrounding the creation of the fresco that still adorns the nave of the church in Saint-Coeur de Marie in the Lac Saint-Jean region of Québec. That fresco depicting the Virgin Mary's ascension was my first encounter with art, with a foreigner and with lies.

In order to portray that fresco, I became a liar and the people from my village became saints and martyrs, artists and models, lovers and misanthropes. I presented their legends the way a flea market hawker displays sacred objects that have been stolen and disguised for resale.

The Madonna Painter or The Birth of a Painting is writ in scarlet pigments, in holy wine and haemoglobin, all the shades of red that flow through us, from our sex to our souls. It is a collision of ecstasies, a bouquet of lies disguised as a fable.

— MICHEL MARC BOUCHARD

The first version of this play was written in the spring of 2002 during a residency at Teatro della Limonaia de Sesto Fiorentino in Florence, Italy. In June 2002, that same theatre company presented a staged reading of the play, translated into Italian and directed by Barbara Nativi. The play was awarded the Primo Arte Candoni 2002 for the best new foreign-language play presented in Italy that year.

Madame Nativi's artistic vision and the work of her company had a deep influence on this play, as did the Madonnas that adorn the walls of Florence.

The Florentine version (published in Italian by Ubulibri, Milan) was first presented in a full production at Teatro della Limonaia in November 2003, and remounted at the Teatro Vittoria in Rome.

The play was first presented in the original French (in the Montreal version) at Théâtre Espace Go in Montreal in April 2004, in a production directed by Serge Denoncourt, assisted by Geneviève Lagacé, with set design by Guillaume Lord, costumes by Ginette Noiseux, lighting by Martin Labrecque, sound design by Stéphane Richard, projections by Martin Gagné, props by Normand Blais, makeup by Jacques-Lee Pelletier, and with the following cast: Annie Charland, Eveline Gélinas, Caroline Lavigne, Evelyne Rompré, Germain Houde, Giorgio Lupano, Olivier Morin and Renaud Paradis.

The playwright wishes to acknowledge the support of Ministère de la Culture du Québec, Conseil des arts et des lettres du Québec, Ministère des relations internationales du Québec, English Theatre of the National Arts Centre in Ottawa and l'Agence culturelle du Québec in Rome.

The play was shortlisted for the 2004 Masque for best play of the year, awarded by l'Académie québécoise du théâtre.

This most recent version of the play was established by the author in collaboration with his English-language translator, Linda Gaboriau, during a residency at the Banff Playwrights Colony in Alberta (Canada) in May 2008.

The English premiere of *The Madonna Painter* was produced by Factory Theatre, Toronto, Ontario, under the artistic direction of Ken Gass, with the participation of Iris Turcott, dramaturge. Its opening night took place on November 19, 2009 with the following cast and crew:

YOUNG PRIEST . . . . Marc Bendavid
ALESSANDRO . . . . Juan Chioran
MARY LOUISE . . . . . . Nicola Correia-Damude
DOCTOR . . . . Brian Dooley
MARY FRANCES . . . . Miranda Edwards
MARY ANNE . . . . Shannon Taylor
MARY OF THE SECRETS . . . . Jenny Young

Director: Eda Holmes
Assistant Director: Cory O'Brien
Set & Costume Designer: Sue LePage
Lighting Designer: Beth Kates
Sound Designer: Reza Jacobs
Stage Manager: Marinda de Beer
Apprentice Stage Manager: Neha Ross

CHARACTERS

MARY FRANCES, *a young woman from the village*

MARY ANNE, *a young woman from the village*

MARY LOUISE, *a young woman from the village*

YOUNG PRIEST

DOCTOR

MARY OF THE SECRETS, *a young woman from the village*

ALESSANDRO, *the Italian painter*

The action takes place in Saint-Coeur de Marie, Lac Saint-Jean, Québec. Fall 1918.

PROLOGUE

YOUNG PRIEST:
(*reading aloud from a little notebook*) A triptych. It will be a triptych. The central fresco will depict the Blessed Virgin with a halo of stars, standing on a cloud ascending into heaven. She will be dressed in a white robe, belted with a gold cord. A long blue veil will cover her head. On her chest, her sacred heart will be circled by a glorious crown and pierced by a sword; a few drops of her sacred blood will glisten like scarlet pearls. In her left hand, she will be holding a stem of white lilies, and with her right hand, she will bless all of humanity. Her closed lips will seal all secrets and all mysteries. Her eyes will comfort us. A chorus of cherubim will dance above her head.

Tableau 1

MARY FRANCES and MARY ANNE are on the bank of a stream. MARY FRANCES is watching a man bathe. The man is not visible. MARY ANNE has covered her eyes with her hands. She will keep her eyes closed until MARY FRANCES leaves.

MARY ANNE
Has he turned around? (*Beat.*) Answer me!

MARY FRANCES
Not yet.

MARY ANNE
We have to leave.

MARY FRANCES
Wait. He's going to turn around.

MARY ANNE
We don't want to be in the woods when there's a storm on the way. It's dangerous.

MARY FRANCES
There's no storm on the way.

MARY ANNE
I never should have followed you.

MARY FRANCES
He's younger, but not as handsome as the one yesterday.

MARY ANNE
You saw another one yesterday?

MARY FRANCES
I was with Mary Michelle, and the day before the day before yesterday, I was with Mary Blanche. And the one the day before the day before yesterday was really handsome.

MARY ANNE
There are so many of them?

MARY FRANCES
A deserter behind every tree.

MARY ANNE
What's he doing now?

MARY FRANCES
He's washing himself.

MARY ANNE
Is he really naked?

MARY FRANCES
As naked as the day he was born. (*Beat.*) We should make some noise so he'll turn around.

MARY ANNE
If he doesn't turn around, it's a sin of intention. If he does, it's a mortal sin. I never should have followed you, Mary Frances.

MARY FRANCES
How do you think we're going to find a husband? We have to start thinking about that at our age. We can't marry the men who went to war, or the ones who got married so they didn't have to go. The only available men left are the ones hiding around here. And I don't want to wither on the vine like an old fruit.

MARY ANNE
What are you doing?

MARY FRANCES
I'm looking for a branch.

MARY ANNE
Don't you dare!

MARY FRANCES breaks a branch.

MARY FRANCES
There. He turned around.

MARY ANNE
A mortal sin! (*Beat.*) Can you see him? Clearly?

MARY FRANCES
Very clearly.

MARY ANNE
From the front?

MARY FRANCES
From the front, from the back and from all around.

MARY ANNE
Can you see what we're not supposed to see?

MARY FRANCES
Yes.

Beat.

MARY ANNE
Is it true what they say ... ?

MARY FRANCES
(*teasing MARY ANNE*) It's even worse than what they say. You're smart not to look. (*improvising*) It's a strange kind of ... creature ... that's constantly changing.

MARY ANNE
A creature? Constantly changing?

MARY FRANCES
Since he turned around, it's changed several times.
Right now it's like a vegetable, a big vegetable with
long roots. Roots that sway back and forth. A
vegetable with eyes.

MARY ANNE
With eyes?

MARY FRANCES
With long eyelashes that flutter slowly.

MARY ANNE
With long eyelashes?

MARY FRANCES
Now it's a slimy fish with the head of a dog, the wings
of a bird and the legs of a reptile covered in scales.
Keep your eyes closed tight. Now it's turned into
seaweed dancing forbidden dances.

MARY ANNE
I hear thunder.

MARY FRANCES
Now it's a boat with a bright pink bow and larvae as
oarsmen.

MARY ANNE
We have to leave!

MARY FRANCES
Now, it's a scabby wound covered in flies.

MARY ANNE
I'm going to faint.

MARY FRANCES
Now it's a snake with a forked tongue.

MARY ANNE
I'm fainting.

MARY FRANCES
    Its lips are red.

MARY ANNE
    I've fainted.

MARY FRANCES
    I think the creature is about to speak. Yes, it's going
    to say something.

MARY ANNE
    I don't want the creature-man to speak to us. (*Beat.*)
    Tell me what it's saying.

MARY FRANCES
    (*making up "the creature's" words*) "Come here, Mary
    Anne."

MARY ANNE
    What?! It's talking to me?!

MARY FRANCES
    "Come closer, girl. Feel the soft, cool mud beneath
    your feet. I'm not dangerous. My appearance is
    misleading. I was made to look vile, just to hide what
    I have to offer. I am made of tender flesh, warm as a
    summer day, and good for anyone who wants to hold
    me. I am the fright of all virgins, the duty of all wives,
    the regret of all saints. I am God's failure. Come
    closer to me, Mary Anne. Come place your lips on
    my luscious flesh. I want you as my bride."

MARY ANNE
    I'm going to die.

MARY FRANCES
    "Will you take me, Mary Anne?"

MARY ANNE
    I'm dying.

MARY FRANCES
"Say you're mine and I will marry you after the
armistice."

MARY ANNE
I'm dead. (*Beat.*) Say something, Mary Frances! Are
you there?

MARY FRANCES
If you let us leave, Mary Anne swears she will marry
you at the end of the war in Europe.

MARY ANNE
What did you say?!

MARY FRANCES
Say yes. It's our only hope.

MARY ANNE
I can't.

MARY FRANCES
Save us.

Silence.

MARY ANNE
Are you still there, Mary Frances? (*MARY FRANCES
caresses her hair lightly.*) Who is touching me?

MARY FRANCES
(*whispering*) It's the creature-man.

MARY FRANCES caresses her face.

MARY ANNE
Why is it touching me?

MARY FRANCES
Swear that you'll marry him.

MARY ANNE
I don't want it to touch me!

MARY FRANCES
Swear you will! It's our only hope.

MARY ANNE
(*relenting*) I swear I'll marry you. I do. I swear. I swear
on the Catechism. On the Holy Gospel. On the
Bible. On the entire holy library. Yes, I will. I will
marry you as soon as they've signed the armistice.
(*MARY FRANCES runs off, laughing.*) Some day people
will say that Mary Anne was damned on a September
day in 1918.

> The YOUNG PRIEST *enters, carrying a suitcase. He*
> *speaks to MARY ANNE.*

YOUNG PRIEST
Pardon me, young lady. I think I'm lost. Can you
show me the way to Saint-Coeur de Marie? (*Beat.*)
Miss?

> MARY ANNE *finally opens her eyes.*

MARY ANNE
You're handsome!

YOUNG PRIEST
(*intimidated by the compliment*) I'm not used to ...

MARY ANNE
You can also change into a priest?!

YOUNG PRIEST
(*not knowing how to reply*) Never mind. I'll find my own
way. (*He continues on his way.*)

Tableau 2

The YOUNG PRIEST appears at the village square and writes in his notebook.

YOUNG PRIEST

The left panel of the fresco will depict two young women on the bank of a stream. In the distance, a man is bathing, as naked as the day he was born.

MARY LOUISE enters, carrying a big basket of bed linen and she will examine the sheets carefully, one by one. The YOUNG PRIEST observes her.

MARY LOUISE

(*reading the first white sheet*) The man and the woman keep their distance. A marriage of convenience. For a dowry or a lot of land. Very little movement. All perfectly calm. The wrinkles are rare, a few in the middle. And they're short. Except for one long crease that's intriguing. The man's body hair is soft and very curly. Her hair is long. She has an ample bosom. And he has broad shoulders. They are young. No trace of saliva. No trace of sweat. No improper secretions. Nothing. Young and dry already. None of the usual creases left by a man who snores and tosses and turns. No talking in their dreams. Dry and silent. (*She sniffs the sheet.*) No eau de cologne. Not even the smell of the horse that brought them here. Dry, silent and odourless. Just this one long intriguing crease across the middle. The man's arm reached out to the woman. That's it, he tried to touch her. He reached out to her in his sleep, in spite of himself. A necessary contact, more powerful than both of them. If I judge by the depth of the crease, his arm remained close to her for a good half hour. I predict that they will remain faithful. (*She rolls the sheet up into a ball and chooses another one.*) Here we have the usual signs of old age. The bones in the knees, the pelvis, the elbows and the skull are very pronounced. He sleeps curled up like a baby. Death is near. (*She rolls up the sheet.*)

YOUNG PRIEST

(*taking notes*) The panel on the right will depict a woman contemplating an immaculate shroud.

MARY LOUISE

(*She reads another sheet.*) He gripped the sheets in his fists. Lots of little wrinkles. Agitated sleep. The body tossed and turned, again and again. The smell of seminary soap. A young priest. He arrived last night on a mission. I see a great project.

TABLEAU 3

At the DOCTOR's house. The YOUNG PRIEST is alone. We can hear the terrible cries of a man suffering in another room. On a table before the YOUNG PRIEST, bloody packages wrapped in butcher's paper. The DOCTOR appears with blood on his hands. He places another package on the table.

DOCTOR
Gangrene. Not a pretty sight.

YOUNG PRIEST
I should have announced my visit.

DOCTOR
I'd already amputated his foot. Now it's his arm.

YOUNG PRIEST
I should have chosen a better time.

DOCTOR
He's a glutton for morphine. He's ready to lose another limb just to get more. Another fiend like him, and my supply is finished.

YOUNG PRIEST
(*looking at the bloody packages on the table*) We must bury that in consecrated ground.

DOCTOR
Your predecessor was much less scrupulous and his dog was fat as a pig.

He moves closer and touches the YOUNG PRIEST's face,
as if examining it.

YOUNG PRIEST
I don't know much about my predecessor ... Why are
you looking at me like that?

DOCTOR
You're too handsome to be a priest.

YOUNG PRIEST
It would be false humility to deny it and vanity to
agree. I am a servant of God.

DOCTOR
In a country where there are no eligible men, it's not
good for a man to be too handsome, especially a
priest. May I pour you a drink?

YOUNG PRIEST
I came to talk to you about a great project.

DOCTOR
Just a little shot?

YOUNG PRIEST
No thank you. I don't drink.

DOCTOR
Just to muss up your face a bit. (*He pours two glasses.*)
Cheers.

YOUNG PRIEST
If you insist. Yes. Cheers. (*to himself, almost speaking in
the voice of the devil*) Alcohol. (*He shudders, then in his
usual voice:*) What are we drinking?

DOCTOR
You don't want to know.

YOUNG PRIEST
Is it homemade?

DOCTOR
You might say so. (*scrutinizing his face*) You really are
too handsome. It's quite a shock. A violent shock. Is
it the communion wafers that make you so fair?

YOUNG PRIEST
Pardon me?

DOCTOR
Is it the communion wine that gives you those rosy
cheeks?

YOUNG PRIEST
I'm afraid I ...

DOCTOR
There aren't many young men left around here. It's
good to see such a healthy specimen.

YOUNG PRIEST
May I explain the reason for my visit?

DOCTOR
Good bone structure ... Healthy muscles. And lips
that would make the whores in the capital green with
envy.

YOUNG PRIEST
I'm not sure how to take that compliment ...

DOCTOR
Such delicate beauty, one could mistake you for a
woman. And your robe could add to the confusion.

YOUNG PRIEST
Really ... I ...

The DOCTOR fills their glasses again.

DOCTOR
Another drink?

YOUNG PRIEST

If you insist … (*more cries of pain from the adjacent room*)
I received some distressing news from the
neighbouring town. They say a dreadful plague is
decimating the communities it strikes. They say the
English Canadian soldiers who've come back from
the European front are to blame. Apparently they've
been spreading the sickness in their search for
French Canadian deserters. They're calling it the
Spanish flu because it has decimated part of the
Spanish royal family. I've done some research.

DOCTOR

(*slamming his fist on the table*) You are the first healthy
body I've seen in weeks and you're telling me about
an epidemic! Talk to me about something else!

YOUNG PRIEST

Perhaps I should have announced my visit?

DOCTOR

Tell me about the confessions you hear. Give me the
juiciest details. Put a bit of joy into my day. (*pouring
him another drink*) Cheers!

YOUNG PRIEST

(*politely*) Yes. Yes. Of course. Cheers.

DOCTOR

(*referring to the YOUNG PRIEST*) Such a frail neck could
snap with a single blow.

YOUNG PRIEST

The epidemic could reach us within weeks.

DOCTOR

Some day, whenever you're ready, I'd like to do your
autopsy.

YOUNG PRIEST

(*not sure how to respond*) Yes, of course.

DOCTOR
It would be a privilege.

YOUNG PRIEST
My head is spinning.

DOCTOR
Spin, Father, spin.

YOUNG PRIEST
(*trying to get back to the point of his visit*) This flu is
devastating and they don't know how to cure it.

DOCTOR
Another drink?

YOUNG PRIEST
If you'll listen to what I'm trying to say.

DOCTOR
What can a country doctor do to fight your flu?

YOUNG PRIEST
Faith, doctor. Faith can bring us great solace.

DOCTOR
(*sarcastically*) Faith?

YOUNG PRIEST
Throughout the history of humanity, the faithful
have tried to avert the worst epidemics by making
offerings to God.

DOCTOR
Two hairs on his chin and he's talking about the
history of humanity.

YOUNG PRIEST
In the fourteenth century, the plague was
transmitted from port to port by sailors. Alexandria,
Cypress, Venice, Marseille. Europe lost a third of its
population. I've done some research. Take cholera
in the nineteenth century. Calcutta, China, Persia,

Africa. In the thirteenth century, a group of fanatics appeared in Italy. They were called the Flagellants. They inflicted all sorts of physical suffering upon themselves to expiate their sins and avert the wrath of God.

DOCTOR

Your eyes are shining.

YOUNG PRIEST

Others were less extreme in their approach. They erected shrines and decorated them with great frescos and rich ornaments. I'm expressing my ideas a bit pell-mell. These are notes for my Sunday sermon. It will be my first sermon. I have to convince the congregation. I have to convince them. (*anxiously*) Why are you looking at me like that? (*Brief silence. He resumes with renewed enthusiasm.*) The neighbouring parishes have some wonderful projects. One of them is going to donate their old chapel to a local Indian reservation. They're going to build a barge, slide the building onto it and sail it across the lake to the Natives. God's house floating on the waters. A white chapel, lit by torches, floating across the water. With the cross on the steeple, pointing to the heavens like a glorious sword. Oarsmen dressed in buckskin, with feather headdresses. There will be hymns … It will be beautiful. And I have a grand idea for our parish. The walls of our church are dreary. The Stations of the Cross are sad.

DOCTOR

What do you expect? It wasn't Jesus' happiest moment.

YOUNG PRIEST

I mean the presentation is sad. It's our duty to illustrate our faith with grandeur and glory. That's how I'm going to present my project on Sunday. "Grandeur and glory."

DOCTOR
Your eyes ... There's something in your eyes.

YOUNG PRIEST
My plan is to adorn our church with a grand fresco depicting the Sacred Heart of the Virgin Mary, the patron saint of our village. I've been corresponding with one of my colleagues, a priest in the next county over. He has written to me about an Italian painter travelling through these parts. He painted a very beautiful Madonna for their sacristy. Apparently he always uses a local girl as a model. That's what makes his work original. I intend to get in touch with him. (*He takes his notebook out from under his cassock.*) I have a lot of ideas for the fresco. When I went to Rome, I saw so many Madonnas ... (*hoping to impress him*) I've been to Rome. I've seen the Pope. (*The DOCTOR doesn't seem remotely impressed.*)

DOCTOR
What does all that have to do with me?

YOUNG PRIEST
(*getting directly to the point*) They say you're the richest man around here.

DOCTOR
That's what they say.

YOUNG PRIEST
They say the notary is a penny-pincher, that the mayor is a miser, that the farmers hoard their money for the afterlife. You are my only hope.

DOCTOR
Your only hope?

YOUNG PRIEST
    I believe it is your Christian duty to donate this work
    of art to our church. Come the Last Judgement, God
    will reward you.

DOCTOR
    Will God put that in writing for me?

YOUNG PRIEST
    I don't know you very well, I haven't heard your
    confession yet—

DOCTOR
    I'd be delighted to whisper my thoughts into such a
    pretty ear.

YOUNG PRIEST
    I think this gift could ease your conscience.

DOCTOR
    Bring your ear closer, Father. (*He leans towards the
    YOUNG PRIEST.*) For a pittance, I deliver women who
    churn out dozens of children. I walk for hours in the
    snow to poison cancer patients who pay me with
    their spittle. For a sea of tears, I abort silly geese who
    were impregnated with lies. I release hanged men
    who pay me with their rope. I predict death and I
    announce it for crusts of bread. That is the extent of
    my wealth and all I have to confess. I don't have the
    slightest stain on my conscience.

YOUNG PRIEST
    What about faith? If only you knew the strength it
    can bring those who carry it within them.

DOCTOR
    I'll spread it out with your guts the day of your
    autopsy.

YOUNG PRIEST
    Faith is immaterial.

DOCTOR
Immaterial. Of course. And in the meantime, I'm the
one who'll pay for the fresco?

*The DOCTOR tears a ring off the dying man's amputated
hand and gives it to the YOUNG PRIEST.*

YOUNG PRIEST
(*horrified*) I can't accept this ring.

DOCTOR
Why not?

YOUNG PRIEST
(*appalled*) You just took it off that amputated hand.

DOCTOR
That's my wages for today. Take it. (*offering him the
ring again*) For the fresco. The rest will follow.

YOUNG PRIEST
(*realizing, delighted*) You agree to pay for it?

DOCTOR
I'm accustomed to flesh turned grey from tobacco,
wizened from the meals of the poor, flabby from too
much fat, yellow from cirrhosis. Flesh like yours is a
sight for sore eyes.

The YOUNG PRIEST reaches out to take his hands.

YOUNG PRIEST
Thank you! Thank you, doctor!

*MARY OF THE SECRETS appears from the adjoining
room. Her face is not visible. Her voice is gentle but sad.*

MARY OF THE SECRETS
You can dispose of the body now.

DOCTOR
Finished?

MARY OF THE SECRETS
Yes.

DOCTOR
He's dead?

MARY OF THE SECRETS
That's what I just said.

DOCTOR
Was it easy?

MARY OF THE SECRETS
No. I sat there for hours and hours, repeating: "Look at me. Take my hand. Everything is better in the other world. Look at me now and let go."

YOUNG PRIEST
Are you the one they call Mary of the Secrets?

MARY OF THE SECRETS
Yes.

YOUNG PRIEST
Your reputation has gone beyond this village. They say you have a gift for delivering the dying from their suffering.

MARY OF THE SECRETS
I receive the secrets that prevent them from departing. They tell me things they have never told anyone.

YOUNG PRIEST
I want to see you at the rectory this week.

MARY OF THE SECRETS
I didn't ask for this, Father. It's a gift.

YOUNG PRIEST
That man dying of gangrene needed me. I was right here in the next room. He should have received the

sacrament of extreme unction and you are the one
who did my job?

DOCTOR
Your predecessor had already "extreme-unctioned"
him three times. He thrived on morphine and holy
oil.

YOUNG PRIEST
If you persist in your stubbornness, I'll have to take
action. (*MARY OF THE SECRETS exits.*)

Pure charlatanism!

DOCTOR
Our world went 'round before your arrival, Father,
and this world will continue to go 'round as it has ...
or no Madonna.

YOUNG PRIEST
What?

DOCTOR
A Madonna ... and perhaps we could add a brand-
new Stations of the Cross.

YOUNG PRIEST
I don't know ...

DOCTOR
A joyful one.

TABLEAU 4

MARY OF THE SECRETS is kneeling in the middle of the field of secrets. Her head buried in a furrow of earth, she is whispering frightful words. A murmuring rises from the depths of the earth, the lament of buried souls. She will repeat the following lines like a litany.

MARY OF THE SECRETS
I curse you. I curse you for all eternity. Go expiate in the bowels of the earth all the pain you caused your kin.

The murmuring ceases.

YOUNG PRIEST
Forgive me for following you. I apologize for my behaviour this morning. I never drink. I know I sound like a drunk who beats his children, trying to make excuses ... but I am a gentle man. I truly regret my attitude. I don't want to become like my superiors.

MARY OF THE SECRETS
Please leave!

YOUNG PRIEST
Why doesn't anything grow in this field?

MARY OF THE SECRETS
(*She ignores him and resumes her litany.*) I curse you. I curse you for all eternity. Go expiate in the bowels of the earth all the pain you caused your kin.

YOUNG PRIEST
You can tell me about your gift. I'm new here. It's my duty to get to know all my parishioners. And since my arrival, everything here eludes me. I can't grasp the local customs.

> *MARY ANNE appears, having followed the YOUNG PRIEST.*

MARY ANNE
There you are. I've been looking for you.

YOUNG PRIEST
Looking for me?

MARY ANNE
I wanted to see if you've changed body.

YOUNG PRIEST
I'll have this body forever and I've donned this robe for eternity.

MARY ANNE
(*not sure she can believe him*) Uh ... We shouldn't stay here.

MARY OF THE SECRETS
She's right.

MARY ANNE
(*whispering*) It's an unholy place.

MARY OF THE SECRETS
She's right.

YOUNG PRIEST
I just wanted to know the nature of her gift.

MARY ANNE
(*surprised by the YOUNG PRIEST's interest in MARY OF THE SECRETS*) We became aware of her powers when her little brother was dying. Ever since his birth, the boy had been suspended over his bed with only his toes

and his forehead touching. A contraption worthy of the instruments of torture from the most glorious chapters of the Inquisition made this feat possible. One day, Mary of the Secrets received permission to visit him. They had always forbidden her to see him, for fear that the sight of her suspended brother would traumatize her. She asked to be left alone with him. She closed the door behind her and an hour later, he was released from his rigging, lying face down, a smile on his lips, dead at last. Everything her little brother told her is buried here in the field of secrets.

MARY OF THE SECRETS
(*to the furrow*) May the earth bury your sins. Silence your unholy secrets.

MARY ANNE
Then there was her old uncle who'd been dying for ages. What he confided to her is buried over there. After that, there was a monk forgotten in his dreary cell since Genesis. His confession, buried nearby, has produced nothing but weeds. And then came her mother's secret ... A dark secret.

YOUNG PRIEST
Do you know what it was?

MARY ANNE
No. No one knows but her.

YOUNG PRIEST
Why do you look so disapproving when you mention it?

MARY ANNE
Because everyone mentions it that way, with a stern face and a serious voice. (*continuing gravely*) She is the guardian of secrets, and should she ever reveal them, those souls would burn in hell.

YOUNG PRIEST
(*unconvinced*) I see.

MARY ANNE
Now people from all the villages around here seek
her services. Those bedridden since the dawn of
time, the elderly with brittle bones, children with the
heads of animals—they all turn to her. And her
father provides her talents for a price.

MARY OF THE SECRETS
Go expiate in the bowels of the earth all the pain you
caused your kin. (*She spits into the furrow and closes it.*)

MARY ANNE
Come, let me take you back to the rectory.

> *MARY ANNE closes her eyes.*

YOUNG PRIEST
You must know the way by heart, if you can lead me
with your eyes closed.

MARY ANNE
I don't want to see you turn into something else. A
slimy fish with the head of a dog, the wings of a bird,
the legs of a reptile covered in scales. No. I don't
want to see that. Give me your hand. I'll introduce
you to the rest of the village.

YOUNG PRIEST
I can hardly wait.

> *The YOUNG PRIEST takes MARY ANNE's hand. They exit.*
> *The murmuring can be heard again and will fade out*
> *when MARY OF THE SECRETS exits.*

TABLEAU 5

The village square in the evening. MARY LOUISE enters,
holding a sheet as if it were the Holy Shroud. She is
clearly waiting for someone. MARY FRANCES joins her.

MARY FRANCES
I came as soon as I could.

MARY LOUISE
(*mysterious*) Never since I began working at the inn
have I seen anything like it.

MARY FRANCES
Tell me ...

MARY LOUISE
In the middle of the night, I was awakened by a
voice, humming a melody. (*She hums a few notes of an*
Italian song.) It was coming from the room next to
mine. A song with words that resembled the
language the priests speak.

MARY FRANCES
Go on.

MARY LOUISE
I threw myself on the floor, face down, my arms
spread out. I thought that in this position I would
certainly understand. If God was singing to me like
this, I must have done something wrong. But I didn't
go dancing, I've been wearing my hat and gloves ...
yet the melody was sweeter than any hymn.

MARY FRANCES
Then what … ?

MARY LOUISE
In the dark of night, a divine song. And then … God
started making strange noises.

MARY FRANCES
Go on.

MARY LOUISE
God blew his nose.

MARY FRANCES
Go on.

MARY LOUISE
God spat.

MARY FRANCES
God spat?

MARY LOUISE
God cleans his teeth.

MARY FRANCES
Wait …

MARY LOUISE
And this morning, God was made man. The
Madonna painter arrived during the night. The
owner of the inn told me he speaks the same
language as the Pope.

MARY FRANCES
Have you seen him?

MARY LOUISE
He'd already gone out when I went to do his room.
The minute I saw his bed, I knew that nothing would
ever be the same.

MARY FRANCES
Tell me what you see!

MARY LOUISE
(*carefully unfolding the sheet, the way one opens a great book*)
Movements like I've never seen from any man from
around here. Perfect curves, complete semi-circles.
Long, languorous stretches. And in the depth of the
creases, I see great virility. And there are all sorts of
new smells. Here, smell. (*They both sniff the sheet,
ecstatically.*)

MARY FRANCES
It smells like gingerbread at Easter!

MARY LOUISE
Yes.

MARY FRANCES
And more than that.

MARY LOUISE
Oranges at Christmas.

MARY FRANCES
Yes.

MARY LOUISE
Chokecherry wine.

MARY FRANCES
Yes.

MARY LOUISE
There's a trace of salt in his sweat.

MARY FRANCES
From the seas he's crossed.

MARY LOUISE
And the smell of tobacco from the West Indies in his
saliva.

MARY FRANCES
Can you imagine spending hours and hours sitting across from a man like that, posing for him without moving?

MARY LOUISE
Being contemplated. And admired.

MARY FRANCES
To feel his presence, in silence. To speak with your eyes alone.

MARY ANNE enters, looking up at the sky. MARY LOUISE hides the sheet.

MARY ANNE
Did you see that?! So many shooting stars!

MARY FRANCES
Good evening, Mary Anne. Are you still mad at me?

MARY ANNE
(*ignoring MARY FRANCES*) Good evening, Mary Louise. This morning they chased an old man out of the village. He was coughing. Coughing blood. (*Silence.*) Have you prepared your presentation for the painter?

MARY LOUISE
(*excited*) I just saw one! I did. I'm making a wish.

They are all looking at the sky.

MARY ANNE
We're supposed to make a wish?

MARY FRANCES
Yes.

MARY ANNE
Well, I have two wishes. I hope the flu will never come here and I hope my fiancé will never turn into anything but a priest. So I'll need two stars.

MARY FRANCES
You're not supposed to tell your wishes.

MARY ANNE
Why?

MARY FRANCES
Because they won't come true.

MARY ANNE
Really?

MARY LOUISE
So you'll have to change your wishes.

MARY ANNE
That's too complicated.

MARY LOUISE
(*to MARY FRANCES*) And you should stop making her believe a lot of nonsense.

MARY ANNE
The priest had me learn a passage from the Bible for my presentation. "The song of songs, which is Solomon's. Let him kiss me with the kisses of his mouth, for thy love is better than wine."

MARY LOUISE
I composed something myself. They say that the woman he chooses as a model will have the most beautiful destiny.

MARY FRANCES
Can you imagine the line-up? Every woman in the village wants to meet him. There'll be Marys as far as the eye can see.

MARY LOUISE
Mary Claire. Mary Martha.

MARY ANNE
Mary Margaret.

MARY FRANCES
Mary Christine.

MARY LOUISE
Mary Evelyn

MARY FRANCES
Even Mary Madeleine.

MARY ANNE
She's missing an eye!

MARY FRANCES
He'll have to paint her profile. (*They laugh.*)

MARY LOUISE
There's Mary Marguerite, too.

MARY FRANCES AND MARY ANNE
She lost both legs!

MARY LOUISE
He'll have to paint some legs for her. (*They laugh even harder.*)

MARY FRANCES
And the twin Marys?

MARY LOUISE
He can't choose one without frustrating the other.

MARY FRANCES
There are more dangerous rivals.

MARY ANNE AND MARY LOUISE
Mary Ellen!

MARY FRANCES
She has such long eyelashes.

MARY LOUISE
Long hair.

MARY ANNE
Long legs.

MARY LOUISE
Everything about her is long.

MARY ANNE
(*joyfully, as she sees a shooting star*) I saw one! (*She makes a wish.*) I want to be the Madonna.

MARY LOUISE
You're not supposed to tell your wish.

MARY ANNE
(*disappointed*) Ohhhhhhhhh ...

MARY FRANCES
Look! It's him. Here he comes.

> *MARY LOUISE and MARY FRANCES check their appearance and stifle nervous laughter. The PAINTER enters with his sketchbook. He greets them politely, speaking more specifically to MARY LOUISE.*

PAINTER
Buona sera!

> *The girls greet the PAINTER in an awkward attempt at Italian. He exits, leaving the girls to swoon.*

MARY LOUISE
Gingerbread at Easter.

MARY FRANCES
Tobacco from the West Indies.

MARY LOUISE
Did you see the scar on his cheek?

MARY FRANCES
Certainly the result of a battle for a woman's heart.

MARY ANNE
(*intrigued by MARY FRANCES's comment*) Ah!

MARY LOUISE
He said "Buona sera" to me.

MARY FRANCES
(*jealous*) "He said 'Buona sera' to me. 'Buona sera!'"
That doesn't mean a thing. He says "Buona sera" to
everyone. "Buona sera!" That just means he's polite.
"Buona sera!"

> *MARY FRANCES tears the sheet away from MARY LOUISE.*

MARY LOUISE
(*stressing every word*) Give me that sheet!

MARY FRANCES
It's mine now.

MARY LOUISE
Give that sheet back to me. I have to wash it.

MARY FRANCES
Wash it! You can't wash the Holy Shroud!

MARY LOUISE
The sheet!

MARY FRANCES
I'll use it to make my Madonna's veil.

Tableau 6

*Chairs are brought in and a platform is set up in the
middle of the square. The square is decorated with
flowers and garlands. Candles are lit. A scene of happy
excitement. In the distance, girls are singing a
traditional folk song. The PAINTER sits down in the
square and starts sketching. He is joined by the DOCTOR
who enters, holding a small package wrapped in blood-
stained paper.*

DOCTOR

For you, the Artist. I've brought a heart. Very fresh.
Still steaming. A fifteen-year-old girl trampled to
death by a mad horse. I assume there'll be a heart on
the Madonna's chest? Look. (*The PAINTER opens the
package.*) See the vivid colour of the veins, the white
of the aorta. Shiny as a weapon. The soul has left.
Perhaps it was never there. (*The DOCTOR lights a
cigarette.*) The first heart I ever heard beating was my
mother's. A huge, loud-mouthed woman. You should
have heard the noise. Every heartbeat was a shock,
like a thunderclap in December. Curled up inside
her belly, I asked her: Mama, tell me, where is the
soul? Mama, can you show me the way to the soul?
Angry and unable to give me an answer, she opened
her mouth wide and vomited me in a stream of
obscene words. I was born passing through her
heart. I tried to cling to its walls, and like all
children, with my first cry, I had already torn

mother's heart apart. I turned to my sisters: Tell me, where is the soul? To answer my question, they'd hold my head against their mammoth breasts. And just as one was about to answer, another would tear me from her arms. The first sister's heart beat to the tune of envy. A shrill, rapid sound. The second one's heart throbbed with jealousy. A plaintive, penetrating sound. The third one thumped with hypocrisy. A dull and sneaky beat. I never managed to find this thing that had been lauded since time immemorial, the delicate haze, the shining aura, the cloud free of all suffering, the pillar of God's house: the soul. When I reached the age where a man takes a wife, I studied medicine. One evening, in the autopsy room, I found myself alone with the cadaver of a young nun. Stripped of her black shell, she offered herself to me like a goddess. Such silent, meditative flesh. I was totally seduced by this woman whose heart had ceased to beat. I paced back and forth until night fell. I locked myself in with her, and like a bridegroom preparing for a wedding night, I undressed, slowly, ceremoniously. I lay down on her cold leather. Is there anything more fascinating than flesh that cannot be marred by time? A frozen image you can admire without fearing that it will wilt or be obscured by some unwelcome memory or disfigured by the scars of history. I whispered fine words in her ear. I covered her with kisses. I ejaculated a resurrection for her. My seed rushed through her veins like a summer squall and her heart began to beat again. She flushed pink and shouted her pleasure. Then, I asked her: Where is the soul? Here or in the hereafter? Inside us or in the unreal? I withdrew and her heart stopped beating again.

PAINTER
Io non capisco.

DOCTOR
> I envy you being able to paint. I envy you being able
> to imagine. I want to see the soul, I want to look it in
> the eye. Not long ago, I thought I'd caught a
> glimpse … briefly. (*He passes the PAINTER a slip of paper.*)
> This is the name of the model you should paint.

> > *The PAINTER reads and stares at the DOCTOR,*
> > *uncomprehendingly.*

> > *The YOUNG PRIEST appears.*

YOUNG PRIEST
> Oh, Doctor!

DOCTOR
> Father!

YOUNG PRIEST
> I simply don't understand the strange feeling that
> comes over me whenever I see you. In theory, your
> presence should be reassuring. (*to the PAINTER who is
> clearly confused*) I see that you have met our doctor?
> Our patron. Don't worry, you'll recover. (*Referring to
> the package containing the heart, disturbed by the blood on the
> paper.*) A local delicacy?

DOCTOR
> (*impatient*) Shall we begin? I have a forceps delivery
> waiting for me.

YOUNG PRIEST
> (*as he continues to set up chairs*) The Gospels present a
> fragmentary view of Mary's life. According to my
> research, Saint Luke mentions her twelve times,
> Saint Matthew, five times, there's one reference in
> Saint Mark, and two in the Gospel according to Saint
> John. Saint Luke describes her as the virgin wife of
> Joseph and tells the famous story of the
> Annunciation, and Saint Matthew, the story of her

flight into Egypt. Saint John mentions her at the wedding in Cana …

DOCTOR

(*taking a flask out of his pocket*) Would our artist like a little drink?

YOUNG PRIEST

Say no … Saint Mark simply names her as Christ's mother. In 431, the Synod of Ephesus names her Mother of God. In 680, Rome consecrates her as Immaculate.

DOCTOR

A little drink for you, Father?

YOUNG PRIEST

Thank you all the same … We had to wait for Pope Sixtus IV to clarify the concept of the Immaculate Conception.

DOCTOR

Let's get on with the presentations.

YOUNG PRIEST

Our artist has to understand his subject.

DOCTOR

When beauty is too talkative, it becomes boring.

YOUNG PRIEST

Are you speaking to me?

DOCTOR

Who else?

YOUNG PRIEST

(*to the PAINTER*) Give me your hands. (*He kisses them.*) They are blessed. I'm sure. They are blessed. Let's begin. Girls have come from all over the parish. One of them sings like a nightingale, another makes the finest lace—

DOCTOR
Let's get started!

YOUNG PRIEST
Yes, let's begin. (*to the young women*) Silence, girls!
This is a solemn occasion. Contemplation is
preferable to agitation. Beware, those chosen by
God, envy and vanity will bring bad counsel. Our
artist wants you to be as authentic as possible. (*to the
PAINTER*) We want authenticity and good taste. Buon
gusto! (*to the young women again*) Perhaps you wonder
what I mean by authenticity? Authenticity is a state of
mind—

DOCTOR
(*impatient*) Father!

YOUNG PRIEST
Yes, of course. Mary Louise, please step forward.
(*MARY LOUISE comes forward.*) This work will demand
great patience on the part of the young woman who
is chosen. She will have to stand for hours, in a
virginal pose, without moving. She will have to
imagine cherubim and seraphim dancing over her
head—

DOCTOR
(*exasperated*) I'm leaving!

YOUNG PRIEST
(*to MARY LOUISE*) Please begin.

MARY LOUISE
(*She strikes a virginal pose. Candid, speaking too fast:*) "The
Virgin's Sheets. They are as immaculate as her soul.
They are embroidered in the gold of her crown and
the blue of the heavens. On the blessed bed, Gabriel,
the Messenger, has left behind a few feathers that
flutter in the wind … that flutter in the wind … "
(*She has a memory lapse.*)

YOUNG PRIEST
"… that flutter in the wind."

Beat.

MARY LOUISE
"… that flutter in the wind … "

Beat.

EVERYONE EXCEPT MARY LOUISE
"… that flutter in the wind … "

MARY LOUISE
(*resuming*) "Gabriel's wings left huge circles that
spread beyond the edges of the sheets. The blessed
bed also welcomed Joseph and the Holy Spirit.
Joseph left the hollow of his back bent from too
much humility and—"

DOCTOR
A virgin with a bosom like that will produce an obese
Jesus. Next!

YOUNG PRIEST
(*calling the next candidate*) Mary Anne! (*to the PAINTER*)
A very strong contender. Wait till you see her. Drawn
by angels. (*MARY ANNE enters.*)

DOCTOR
The angels ran out of ink.

YOUNG PRIEST
She is going to recite the Song of Solomon for us
and—

DOCTOR
We'll be here till midnight.

YOUNG PRIEST
… and Lamentations.

DOCTOR

I can hear those of my forceps delivery.

MARY ANNE

(*Striking a pose. She can hardly speak and her elocution is grotesque.*) "The song of songs, which is Solomon's. Let him kiss me with the kisses of his mouth, for thy love is better than wine." My tongue is sticking to the roof of my mouth.

YOUNG PRIEST

What did she say?

DOCTOR

(*imitating MARY ANNE's elocution*) Her tongue is sticking to the roof of her mouth.

MARY ANNE

Too nervous.

YOUNG PRIEST

What?

DOCTOR

(*laughing loudly, he repeats MARY ANNE's words*) "Too nervous!"

MARY ANNE

I've got no saliva.

YOUNG PRIEST

Salivate, my dear. Salivate.

MARY ANNE

My legs are going to give out.

YOUNG PRIEST

Salivate.

MARY ANNE

My legs are giving out.

YOUNG PRIEST

The Song!

MARY ANNE
    My legs have given out.

    She collapses.

YOUNG PRIEST
    I helped her rehearse her text.

DOCTOR
    (*laughing heartily*) Go ahead, Father, recite it for her!

    MARY ANNE pulls herself to her feet, determined, and strikes her pose again.

MARY ANNE
    (*still grappling with her problem*) "The song of songs, which is Solomon's. Let him kiss me with the kisses of his mouth … "

DOCTOR
    I refuse to pay for such a terrified Madonna!

    MARY ANNE exits in tears.

YOUNG PRIEST
    It's very nerve-wracking for the young women. Now I can't remember who's next.

    MARY FRANCES enters, wearing the veil made from the YOUNG PRIEST's sheet.

MARY FRANCES
    (*striking a rather provocative pose*) I'm Mary Frances.

YOUNG PRIEST
    You are not on my list.

MARY FRANCES
    My father could appeal to the diocese.

YOUNG PRIEST
    Let him appeal. I'm sure the bishop would be delighted to hear your confession. I inquired about

your berry-picking escapades in the woods and I am convinced that the Virgin Mary does not partake of that jam.

MARY FRANCES
(*ignoring the YOUNG PRIEST*) Buon giorno, Alessandro. Is that how you pronounce your name? Alessandro? How is my accent? I've heard all sorts of things about Italian men. Apparently you haven't all taken vows to become the Pope. (*She moves closer to him and hums the Italian song heard earlier. MARY OF THE SECRETS appears at the edge of the square during the song.*)

PAINTER
Venite un po avanti.

MARY FRANCES
(*beaming*) What did he say to me?

YOUNG PRIEST
He asked you to come closer.

MARY FRANCES
(*to the PAINTER*) As close as you want.

PAINTER
(*indicating MARY OF THE SECRETS*) Dicevo alla ragazza che é appena entrata.

YOUNG PRIEST
(*indicating MARY OF THE SECRETS*) He's speaking to her.

MARY FRANCES
To who?

PAINTER
Uscite dall'ombra, signorina.

> *Everyone turns to MARY OF THE SECRETS as she steps out of the shadows.*

MARY OF THE SECRETS
The priest said he wanted to see me.

PAINTER
Veneti avanti.

YOUNG PRIEST
Mary of the Secrets isn't on the list.

PAINTER
Mettetevi in luce.

MARY FRANCES
We just told you, she's not on the list.

MARY OF THE SECRETS
The priest asked me to come see him.

PAINTER
Venite avanti. (*MARY OF THE SECRETS moves into the light shyly.*) Alzate un po la testa.

MARY OF THE SECRETS
What?

PAINTER
Aspettate. (*He goes to place her head in the desired pose.*)

MARY OF THE SECRETS
What is he doing?

PAINTER
Unite le mani. (*He places her hands together.*)

MARY OF THE SECRETS
Why does he want me to do this?

PAINTER
Cosa avete sulle labbra? (*He passes his finger over the lips of MARY OF THE SECRETS.*) Della terra?

MARY FRANCES
Careful! She bites!

MARY OF THE SECRETS
(*rubbing her eyes*) The sun hurts my eyes.

PAINTER
Lasciate che le lacrime scorrano. (*He wipes her tears.*)
Sono insperate. (*to MARY FRANCES*) Datemi il vostro
velo.

MARY FRANCES
What does he want?

YOUNG PRIEST
He wants your veil.

> The PAINTER *takes MARY FRANCES's veil and places it
> on the head of MARY OF THE SECRETS.*

PAINTER
Mandate via tutte le altre.

YOUNG PRIEST
(*gravely*) You're making a hasty choice. I'm sure Mary
Anne has had time to salivate.

MARY FRANCES
(*tearing her shawl away from MARY OF THE SECRETS*) Our
Madonna of the Corpses! With your phoney gifts!
Your little brother, the Martyr, hadn't made a sound
for years when you went into his room. Not a sound.
When he tried to open his jaw to speak to you, the
effort killed him. A grimace turned into a smile. A
coincidence disguised as a miracle.

MARY OF THE SECRETS
I just came to see the priest.

PAINTER
Voglio restare solo con lei.

YOUNG PRIEST
We can't leave them alone like this. They need a
chaperone.

MARY FRANCES
A chaperone! Death is her chaperone.

MARY FRANCES exits.

YOUNG PRIEST
(*to the PAINTER*) I don't know how I'll explain your
choice to the villagers. I'll have to find the right
words.

DOCTOR
(*speaking under his breath to the PAINTER*) What do you
think you're doing? If the Madonna doesn't have the
face I chose, you won't get your salary! (*He exits.*)

*The YOUNG PRIEST moves his chair closer to the
PAINTER and MARY OF THE SECRETS. He will play
chaperone. Beat. He crosses himself. His face lights up.*

YOUNG PRIEST
We have our model. (*to MARY OF THE SECRETS, like a
prayer*) Blessed art thou, young woman. You have
been chosen for a great joy. A new destiny can be
yours. You are the world's salvation. Full of grace.
Blessed art thou, amongst women.

MARY OF THE SECRETS
(*to the PAINTER*) Why are you looking at me like that?
Why upset my unhappy fate? I've made my peace
with unhappiness. Unhappiness brings no surprises.

YOUNG PRIEST
You will wear the crown!

MARY OF THE SECRETS
Why overwhelm me with joys that will only be
destroyed? (*She withdraws to the shadows.*) Light reveals
our vanities.

PAINTER
Splendida.

MARY OF THE SECRETS
> Why do the demons enjoy tormenting me like this?
> Their sweet promises of springtime will distract me
> and I'll forget the secrets buried in silence. They'll
> turn into handsome young men whispering gentle
> words. But autumn will bring tears and the young
> men will grow horns and I'll vomit remorse.

PAINTER
> Siete molto bella e la tristezza vi fa da aureola.

YOUNG PRIEST
> You are truly beautiful. You wear your sadness like a
> halo.

MARY OF THE SECRETS
> (*to the PAINTER*) I know all the stories. All the refrains.
> Hell awaits us all. Nothing else. Better to die in our
> mother's womb. I don't like the look in your eyes.

> *The following speeches of the YOUNG PRIEST and the*
> *PAINTER will be spoken simultaneously.*

PAINTER
> Nei vostri c'è molta grazia.

YOUNG PRIEST
> Yours are full of grace.

MARY OF THE SECRETS
> Only the dying look at me.

PAINTER
> Eppure io sto bene.

YOUNG PRIEST
> But I am in good health.

MARY OF THE SECRETS
> No one from around here speaks to me kindly.

PAINTER
> Io no sono di qui.

YOUNG PRIEST
I am not from around here.

MARY OF THE SECRETS
People around here are afraid of me.

PAINTER
Io non ho paura di nulla.

YOUNG PRIEST
I am afraid of nothing.

MARY OF THE SECRETS
I know everything no one should know.

PAINTER
No sapete nulla di me.

YOUNG PRIEST
You know nothing of me.

MARY OF THE SECRETS
You are robbing me of something with your eyes.

PAINTER
Ci vedremo spesso

YOUNG PRIEST
We'll be seeing a lot of each other.

MARY OF THE SECRETS
I don't think so.

PAINTER
Voi avete la malinconia che cerco.

YOUNG PRIEST
You have the melancholy I've been searching for.

MARY OF THE SECRETS
I have to leave.

PAINTER
Sarà un'Assunzione. Voi meritate l'Assunzione.

YOUNG PRIEST
It will be an Assumption. You deserve an
Assumption.

MARY OF THE SECRETS
I can't stay.

PAINTER
Mary of the Secrets, I have chosen you and you must
stay.

MARY OF THE SECRETS comes back into the light.

YOUNG PRIEST
(*surprised*) You speak our language?

PAINTER
A foreigner's strength lies in his ability to listen to
everything and pretend he understands nothing.

*The PAINTER opens his sketchbook and begins to draw.
The YOUNG PRIEST, delighted, opens the package
containing the heart.*

YOUNG PRIEST
On her breast, a crown of gold will circle her Sacred
Heart.

Tableau 7

MARY LOUISE is carrying a pile of sheets.

MARY LOUISE

He teaches her the names of birds we just called "birds." He has her taste plants we thought were poisonous. He describes the dance of the clouds and tells her how they change name with every movement. He pays her such unusual compliments he has to explain them to her. He told her she is "splendida." I'd love to have someone call me "splendida." (*She unfolds a sparkling white sheet.*) His sheets show signs of more and more agitation. No matter how often I iron them, no matter how hot my iron is, I can't erase the creases. He lies on his bed in the position of a man who is daydreaming. His hands behind his head. His shoulders sink into the cloth. He's thinking of her. He's smiling. Every wrinkle betrays the passion he can barely contain. There are mountains where once there were only hills. Rivers where once there were only streams. The winds of pagan lands blow over his bed.

TABLEAU 8

On the bank of the deserters' stream. MARY ANNE
approaches, in a state of agitation.

MARY ANNE

> (*fearfully*) I shouldn't be in the woods when there's a
> storm on the way. It's dangerous. (*reassuring herself*)
> There's no storm on the way. No storm on the way.
> (*Beat.*) They said we should be able to see the chapel
> float across the water from here. (*We hear the sound of*
> *a man coughing. The sound is strangely amplified.*) Who's
> there? I know there's someone. (*MARY FRANCES comes*
> *out of the woods, buttoning her blouse, rearranging her hair.*)
> Mary Frances? What are you doing here? Who were
> you with?

MARY FRANCES

> No one.

MARY ANNE

> There's blood on your collar. I heard someone
> cough. A man.

MARY FRANCES

> So you've got your answer.

MARY ANNE

> Who was it? They've arrested all the deserters. Who
> was it?

MARY FRANCES

> I don't have to tell you.

MARY ANNE
Was he English?

MARY FRANCES
(*to change the subject*) Don't look!

MARY ANNE
What?

MARY FRANCES
It's back.

MARY ANNE
(*covering her eyes*) The creature?

MARY FRANCES
Don't move.

MARY ANNE
Is it wearing a cassock? Does it have a beautiful face?

MARY FRANCES
Oh, no!

MARY ANNE
A vegetable with eyes? A slimy fish with the head of a dog, the wings of a bird and the legs of a reptile covered in scales?

MARY FRANCES
If you tell anyone you caught me in the woods, it swears it will take the shape of your worst nightmares.

MARY ANNE
I never saw you in the woods! Never!

MARY FRANCES
(*hissing in her ear*) I'll leave you alone with your lover.

    MARY FRANCES exits.

MARY ANNE

>(*scared to death, her eyes still closed*) Don't leave me alone with that! Mary Frances! (*trying to reassure herself*) There's no thunder. No storm on the way. No thunder. No storm on the way. (*Beat.*) I have a fever. The doctor says it begins with a fever, but I refuse to believe him. (*turning back to the creature*) I will marry you. I said I would, and lying is a sin. Look at my hands, they're trembling. I promised I'd be yours and I don't even know your name. I always knew I wouldn't get to choose my husband. That's how it is for women around here. There are no love stories like the ones in the forbidden books, the books we hide under our mattresses. But still, it's not normal, not to know your fiancé's name. At first, you only see his qualities ... and then you really get to know him, but at least you know his name. Turn back into the new priest! I beg you! Become a cassock again! (*She kneels down and joins her hands in prayer.*) I want to understand my sacrifice. Why is God asking me to marry you? Saint Martina was flayed with nails of iron and they poured boiling oil on her wounds. Saint Frances was hanged by the hair. Saint Christina smiled as she gathered up pieces of her torn flesh and offered them to her executioner. Saint Agatha had her breasts cut off. They say that sacrifice makes our faith grow deeper. I'm cold. I have a fever. The doctor says that's how it begins, but I refuse to believe him.

>*The YOUNG PRIEST appears behind MARY ANNE.*

YOUNG PRIEST

>(*speaking to MARY ANNE, from a distance*) They didn't come. Hardly a soul came to see us set God's house afloat.

MARY ANNE
> (*relieved to hear the YOUNG PRIEST's voice*) At last. His
> voice. (*She crosses herself.*)

YOUNG PRIEST
> The crossing took over an hour. They missed a
> beautiful show. It's because of the flu. People are
> afraid of gatherings. Fear is powerful. I should do
> some research. Now they have their chapel over
> there. And we will have our Madonna. (*He comes closer
> to her.*)

MARY ANNE
> Keep talking.

YOUNG PRIEST
> The painter is working very slowly. But we don't want
> a Madonna with vague features. I suppose it takes
> time to create a real work of art.

MARY ANNE
> Please keep talking.

YOUNG PRIEST
> And it takes inspiration. I read somewhere that
> inspiration is impossible to define.

MARY ANNE
> (*She opens her eyes and touches his face.*) How do you
> manage to hide behind such a beautiful face?

YOUNG PRIEST
> Do you feel sick, Mary Anne? You seem feverish.

MARY ANNE
> You have no right to take this shape. No right.

> *She passes out in the YOUNG PRIEST's arms. He holds
> her on his lap, and caresses her face affectionately.*

YOUNG PRIEST

Pearls of dew on her forehead. Such a fragile soul.
Too fragile for these terrible times. (*He caresses her
hair.*) Her breathing seems calmer. We must protect
her. Protect her from the soldiers who are spreading
the plague. They travel from village to village, from
bell tower to bell tower, looking for deserters. They
speak in English and cough in Spanish. Such delicate
hands. It's growing dark. We shouldn't wake her.
We'll let her sleep. What if the plague is already
inside her? No. We'll reassure her. It will go away.
Such pale hands ... It's night already! God retires but
the Devil never sleeps. I'll watch over her. (*He takes
one of MARY ANNE's hands and caresses his own face with it.*)
Such small hands ... (*He cries.*)

MARY OF THE SECRETS

(*as she enters with a long white veil in her hands*) Father?

YOUNG PRIEST

(*embarrassed, feeling as if he's been caught in the act*) She
wasn't feeling well. She collapsed. She's sleeping.
Why are you looking at me like that? She wasn't
feeling well. She collapsed and now she's sleeping.
Why aren't you posing for the painter? Time is of the
essence. Look at poor Mary Anne!

MARY OF THE SECRETS

(*handing him her veil*) I don't want to be the Madonna
anymore.

YOUNG PRIEST

In these days of uncertainty, you could spare us your
capricious moods.

MARY OF THE SECRETS

I don't want to pose for him anymore.

YOUNG PRIEST
All the young women who wanted to play this role
were terribly hurt when they weren't chosen. Show a
bit of respect for them and their disappointment,
and go back to the painter.

MARY OF THE SECRETS
He still hasn't done a single sketch of my face. I'm
not a good model.

YOUNG PRIEST
Your humility is irritating.

MARY OF THE SECRETS
His eyes! You should see his eyes when he's drawing
me.

YOUNG PRIEST
He is searching for something. I imagine that artists
are always searching for something.

MARY OF THE SECRETS
(*searching for the right words*) When he looks at me, the
sky opens up ... And I look at him, again and again,
and I can feel myself rising higher and higher.

YOUNG PRIEST
That is your ascension. That is what he's searching
for.

MARY OF THE SECRETS
When I struggle to come back down to earth,
because I have to come back down to earth, he tells
me to look at him more closely. If you only knew
what I see when he looks at me.

YOUNG PRIEST
I hope he sees as much.

MARY OF THE SECRETS
Please ask him to find another model.

YOUNG PRIEST

I cannot interfere with the creative process.

MARY OF THE SECRETS

I beg you.

YOUNG PRIEST

If you reject your destiny, you will be responsible for many tears.

MARY OF THE SECRETS

I don't know what to think.

YOUNG PRIEST

Stop whining and accept your responsibility. Our hope is in you. Look at poor Mary Anne. Already overcome by the sickness. Once the fresco adorns the nave of our church, we will worship your image and our fears will disappear. Inspire him. Do everything you can to inspire him. If he asks you to pose for him at night, you must remain with him till dawn. If he asks you to hold the pose, you must suffer beyond endurance. If your immobility leaves you thirsty, embrace the desert. If it leaves you famished, embrace famine. If he asks you to fly away, spread your wings. Understand your mission and accomplish it selflessly. Awaken the muses dozing inside you. God has led you away from the dead and dying, Mary of the Secrets. For once, He is asking you to serve the living.

MARY ANNE

(*coming to her senses*) Mary of the Secrets? Already? Have you come to take my soul?

YOUNG PRIEST

(*upset by MARY ANNE's words*) Do everything he asks you! Everything! You must save us!

The PAINTER appears.

PAINTER

(*speaking to* MARY OF THE SECRETS) Why did you run
away?

YOUNG PRIEST

Come, Mary Anne, come with me.

MARY OF THE SECRETS

Don't leave. We need a chaperone.

YOUNG PRIEST

Unfortunately I cannot be in all places, at all times.

> MARY ANNE *and the* PRIEST *exit. The* PAINTER *sits
> down with his sketchbook on his knees and contemplates*
> MARY OF THE SECRETS *who resumes her pose.*

MARY OF THE SECRETS

Last night I woke up because women were reciting
the rosary at my window. I've been finding food,
handiwork, even money, on my doorstep every
morning. People have started coming to me for
miracles and for cures. Remind them that I am only
a model.

PAINTER

You talk too much.

MARY OF THE SECRETS

Can you imagine what would happen if the villagers
found out that you are only drawing clouds,
mountains and fields? Never my face!

PAINTER

When I draw the first feature of your face, it will be
clear.

MARY OF THE SECRETS

Yesterday, I failed with an old woman. She took hours
of effort, hours before she died. I felt like strangling
her to speed things up. This Madonna business is
distracting me. Draw my face.

69

PAINTER
I'm waiting for you to give it to me.

MARY OF THE SECRETS
Here I am, can't you see? *[stand]*

PAINTER
Have you ever loved a man? *slowly*

Beat. *[pause long/fall to the floor]*

MARY OF THE SECRETS
I know I should be afraid of you.

PAINTER
Has a man ever loved you?

MARY OF THE SECRETS
I can't remember. *[hide face in knees]*

PAINTER
Not a single flame?

MARY OF THE SECRETS
Flames don't burn for a woman who blows out the
candles. *[slow face]*

PAINTER
And if I told you—

MARY OF THE SECRETS *[Quick]*
I know all the stories, all the refrains. *[kneel]*

PAINTER
It takes time and patience to understand a face. Its
beauty pales if you look at it without loving it.

He moves closer to her.

MARY OF THE SECRETS *[all]*
Don't touch me. *on the floor again*

PAINTER
What if I promised to take you far away from here?
Away from your legends? Away from your cadavers?

MARY OF THE SECRETS
I know all the words.

PAINTER
If I dazzled you with promises I won't keep? If I
offered to take you across the four seas, to the other
world where young women are betrayed. If I became
your first shipwreck?

He caresses her face gently.

MARY OF THE SECRETS
We don't touch each other like that around here.

PAINTER
The Virgin Mary's most glorious moment came when
they took her son down from the cross. A unique
blend of suffering and beatitude. I want your
beatitude, Mary.

MARY OF THE SECRETS
(*murmuring, confused*) I should leave! Immediately!

PAINTER
Tell me a secret. Just one and I will draw your face.
(*He caresses her neck.*)

MARY OF THE SECRETS
(*stunned*) Men around here don't do what you're
doing.

PAINTER
One day, back in my country, I was working on a
fresco depicting the Multiplication of the Loaves.
Behind Jesus, I had placed a young servant who was
slicing the bread … I had chosen a very beautiful girl
as my model. Light bloomed on her face. I found a
pretext, some necessary finishing touches, so I could

be alone with her. She was so irresistible, it would have been sacrilege not to honour her beauty. I'll tell you the ending if you tell me a secret ...

He takes MARY's hands and kisses them tenderly. She gazes at her hands as if they were the most amazing things she had ever encountered in her life. We hear the murmuring of buried souls.

MARY OF THE SECRETS
Yesterday, I entered that old woman's room. She gestured for me to come closer. Her wizened face ... Her frail hands ... She told me that she could only confess her secret to me, the only woman who receives confessions around here.

PAINTER
Ancora!

MARY OF THE SECRETS
I held her hand. "Look at me. Hold my hand. Everything is better in the other world. Look at me now, and let go." (*imitating the old woman's voice*) "I did something terrible. One day, I kissed a young woman on the lips."

PAINTER
I kissed the girl's lips.

MARY OF THE SECRETS AND THE PAINTER
"I have never forgotten that kiss."

The wind rises in the distance.

MARY OF THE SECRETS
And I started to laugh.

PAINTER
She started to scream and she slashed my face with her knife.

MARY OF THE SECRETS
Then she died.

PAINTER
Then I left the country. (*inviting her to join him in a better world*) "Look at me. Hold my hand. Everything is better in the other world. Look at me now, and let go."

> MARY OF THE SECRETS *and the* PAINTER *kiss, passionately. He spreads her veil on the ground and invites her to lie down beside him. In ecstasy, she releases her secrets.*

MARY OF THE SECRETS
Another woman told me, "I held his little head in the basin of water and I waited until it was over." One man said, "I was the one who stole the poor man's money."

PAINTER
Ancora!

MARY OF THE SECRETS
Another woman said, "One night I slept with my father-in-law." A man told me, "I didn't go to their rescue … "

PAINTER
Ancora!

MARY OF THE SECRETS
And my own mother told me, "Let me tell you why your little brother suffered the way he did. He was a bastard. The son of the dirty beggar who used to sleep on the bench outside the house. When I realized I was carrying his child, I used my knitting needles. To no avail. He was born deformed."

PAINTER
Ti amo, Maria dei Segreti!

The murmuring ceases. The rising wind blows louder.
The lovers kiss and exit. MARY LOUISE enters and picks
up the veil MARY OF THE SECRETS has left behind.

MARY LOUISE

(*sadly*) It's a flag with a gruesome effigy in the centre.
There is neither a doe, nor a lion. Nor a crown. It's
the flag of a lost battle, trampled in the rush of
retreat. Woe unto us all.

The wind blows harder.

TABLEAU 9

At the DOCTOR's house. The DOCTOR pours the first of several drinks for the YOUNG PRIEST. We hear the wind whistling.

DOCTOR
The veil?

YOUNG PRIEST
(*his eyes glowing*) Evanescent.

DOCTOR
The Sacred Heart?

YOUNG PRIEST
Scarlet.

DOCTOR
The stars?

YOUNG PRIEST
Dazzling.

DOCTOR
The crown?

YOUNG PRIEST
Amazing! The clouds and the trompe-l'oeil, very strange. The Halo! The Precious Blood, the Robe, the Golden Belt, the Lilies, the Sword, the Cherubim … he's painted everything!

DOCTOR
>Everything?

YOUNG PRIEST
>(*discouraged*) Everything ... except her face! I think
>you should give him his salary, or at least an advance.
>That might be an incentive. I've been chaperoning
>them for weeks now. They're constantly smiling at
>each other, starting sentences they never finish,
>stifling their laughter. Sometimes I'm so exhausted, I
>fall asleep. In these frightening times, my mission is
>very demanding. When I wake up, they're still there,
>like naughty children trying to hide some mischief.
>And I must confess that I've had to leave them alone
>occasionally. In the past few days I've noticed that
>their lack of concentration is getting worse ... she's
>been vomiting, she's very pale and needs to rest a lot.
>How awful it would be if we lost her, a victim of the
>plague for which we hoped she would bring
>salvation. Oh, Lord! This grand idea of mine ... And
>now this wind that hasn't let up for weeks ...

DOCTOR
>I never noticed that before.

YOUNG PRIEST
>You're right. The wind has never been so constant.

DOCTOR
>No. I'm talking about the wrinkle on your forehead.
>(*insistent, concerned*) It's new. And I don't like it.

YOUNG PRIEST
>We're marking white crosses on doors to identify the
>houses where victims have died of the sickness and
>you're talking to me about a wrinkle on my forehead.

DOCTOR
>And the little crease at the corner of your lips.

YOUNG PRIEST
We have a Madonna who might succumb to the flu
from one day to the next, and you're worrying about
a little crease at the corner of my lips?

DOCTOR
Time is running out.

YOUNG PRIEST
(*emphatically*) Yes. Time is running out.

DOCTOR
I'll give him an advance so he'll finish the face.

YOUNG PRIEST
Yes! That will certainly encourage him!

DOCTOR
Why are you smiling?

YOUNG PRIEST
I'm so glad you're finally taking an interest in my
project.

DOCTOR
It's the first time I've ever made you smile.

YOUNG PRIEST
You just looked at me the way the painter sometimes
does. He turns away from his model and stares at me
the way you just did.

DOCTOR
If it is of any consolation, your Madonna came to see
me. Her nausea has nothing to do with the flu. And
it has nothing to do with the Immaculate
Conception. She's pregnant.

(*The YOUNG PRIEST is flabbergasted, in a state of shock.
Beat.*) Are you all right?

YOUNG PRIEST
And I was the one who pushed her into his arms!

Tableau 10

The ever-present wind. A procession enters, carrying
MARY FRANCES on a stretcher. She is feverish. MARY OF
THE SECRETS enters and people kneel as she passes. We
hear the murmuring of prayers being recited.

MARY FRANCES
Come close to me, Mary of the Secrets.

MARY OF THE SECRETS
Why did you send for me?

MARY FRANCES
Why do people ever send for you?

MARY OF THE SECRETS
I don't have time.

MARY FRANCES
I should hate you, but hatred is always the first thing
to go when a body is in pain.

The PAINTER enters with a painting wrapped in a sheet
under his arm. He goes over to MARY OF THE SECRETS
and takes her hand.

MARY FRANCES
Do you love him?

MARY OF THE SECRETS
Yes.

MARY FRANCES
Tell me, what is love like?

Beat.

MARY OF THE SECRETS
When he's not by my side, I have a fever. When he's
there, I feel faint. When he takes my hand, I want his
lips. When he is naked, I undress him again. I watch
him sleep and I want his children. He picks up a
piece of wood and I want his house. When he enters
me, I want the serpent to live inside me forever. He
makes me feel alive. I am immortal.

MARY FRANCES manages a faint smile.

MARY FRANCES
Has he painted your smile?

MARY OF THE SECRETS
Soon. It will be a surprise.

MARY FRANCES
Come closer, Mary of the Secrets. It's time for me to
tell you my secret. The young English soldier died
coughing, gasping, "Just one kiss." The doctor cut
him into small pieces, exactly the same size. Small,
carefully wrapped packages of my soldier. Even dead
and chopped into pieces, his flesh was still crawling
with the sickness. The doctor asked me to dispose of
it. I threw the packages into the river. We didn't want
the English Canadian soldiers to find the body of
one of their own in a little French Canadian village.
Just one kiss, Mademoiselle. The soldier was lying in
the woods, exhausted from fits of coughing. I lay
down beside him, exhausted from fits of longing. I
brought my face close to his, even though I knew …
my mouth close to his lips … even though I knew …
All kisses should be as beautiful as the one he gave
me—a kiss that makes you cling to life for another

moment. Tears in my eyes, blood on his lips … "Just one kiss. I want just one kiss," he said, "a last kiss." And I said, "More, more." (*She coughs.*) You see, it's his blood that I'm coughing. (*Beat.*) Mary of the Secrets, recite it for me: "Open your eyes. Look at me. Everything is better in the other world. Forget the hardships of this world." (*with the urgency of despair*) Tell me that we don't have to suffer to deserve the other world, tell me there is a God who isn't angry. Tell me that young girls never grow old, that they spend their days singing and dancing, dreaming of beautiful beaux drunk with laughter in the fields. Tell me they write silent letters of longing. Tell me they still find love on the banks of a stream. Give me your hand. Guide me. (*She takes her hand.*)

MARY OF THE SECRETS
 I can't do it.

MARY FRANCES
 I beg you.

MARY OF THE SECRETS
 Let go of my hand.

MARY FRANCES
 Open the gates of heaven.

> *MARY FRANCES dies. MARY OF THE SECRETS exits, terrified, leaving the PAINTER behind. The DOCTOR comes to certify MARY FRANCES's death. He takes a sheet from MARY LOUISE. They wrap MARY FRANCES's body in the sheet and take her away. They begin to tear up other sheets to make masks.*

MARY LOUISE
 (*her arms outstretched, her hands empty*) The epidemic has robbed me of my sheets. They came to take the last one. They wrap the corpses in them and throw them into the common grave. I thought there would

always be men and women who sleep in sheets. I never would have thought that one morning there would be no more sheets. I used to wake up eager to do all the rooms, excited by the prospect of the mysteries awaiting me. I never thought I would have to face the death of those mysteries. (*Suddenly, a sad realization.*) And what will they wrap me in?

The PAINTER goes over to the DOCTOR.

DOCTOR
So, how is your model doing? They say you have made all your Madonnas unhappy.

PAINTER
Should I show you the face?

He unwraps the painting and shows it to the DOCTOR. We can't see the front of the painting.

DOCTOR
It's too beautiful. It's quite a shock. A violent shock. Is there anything more fascinating than flesh that cannot be marred by time? An image you can admire without fearing that it will wilt …

PAINTER
This face will remain young for all eternity.

DOCTOR
Your work is finished. Now mine begins.

PAINTER
Io non capisco. (*The PAINTER starts to wrap up the painting again.*)

DOCTOR
Let me take another look. It's quite a shock. A violent shock. Every time. (*Beat. The PAINTER wraps up the painting.*) Here is your salary. The influenza has

been generous. (*The DOCTOR gives him a handful of jewellery and turns to leave.*)

PAINTER

I thought she was different from the others.

DOCTOR

Who?

PAINTER

She was seduced by every line, like all the others. "You are truly beautiful and you wear your sadness like a halo." "You have the melancholy I've been searching for." "Splendida." Beauty pales when we stare at it too long. Words lose their meaning when we repeat them. Lovers kill love. It's in our nature. Men and women. We are determined to tame everything that mystifies us. We become bored with things that once dazzled us, indifferent to things that once excited us. Ecstasy is cruel and ephemeral. We're always looking for the flaw. I thought she'd give me a real fight. I thought she would resist me. The minute she gave in, she crumbled in my eyes. Her mystery melted like the first snow of winter. I wanted a Madonna who embodied suffering and beatitude. I turned her into a woman who only dreams of ordinary happiness. Soon her eyes will become pleading, her hands monotonous, her lips predictable. Her back no longer stands so straight.

DOCTOR

You'll have to excuse me. I'm off to inaugurate the common grave.

PAINTER

What about the baby?

DOCTOR

If you need my services, you know where to find me.

Tableau 11

*His cassock attached around his hips, the YOUNG
PRIEST bares his back to MARY ANNE who is flagellating
him. She seems to be in a trance.*

MARY ANNE
Expiate, Father! Expiate! (*Whip.*)

YOUNG PRIEST
According to the tenets of the Christian faith, it is
heresy to adore a graven image. Harder! (*Whip.*) It is
heresy to create icons to ward off a plague. (*Whip.*)

MARY ANNE
We will ward off the flu, Father.

YOUNG PRIEST
Harder. (*Whip.*) In early Christianity, it was forbidden
to paint the faces of the saints. Our faith resides in
the invisible. (*Whip.*) God's teachings need no
adornment. No portrait was done of Jesus in his
lifetime. They say he had no beard. That the
orthodox priests of the Middle Ages imposed their
beards on his image. Harder! (*Whip.*) They say that
Saint Luke painted a portrait of the Virgin and it was
destroyed.

MARY ANNE
We are warding off the flu, Father. (*Whip.*)

YOUNG PRIEST

All the images we worship are illusions. (*Whip.*)
Heresy! Art is nothing but heresy! (*Whip, followed by a
cry of pain.*) That's enough, Mary Anne. Enough!

MARY ANNE

We have warded off the flu, Father.

YOUNG PRIEST

(*in pain*) By now, it must have gone back to Spain.
Thank you, Mary Anne.

MARY ANNE

I put all my devotion into it.

YOUNG PRIEST

And your devotion is great, I can feel it.

MARY ANNE

(*pleased*) My arm aches.

YOUNG PRIEST

(*in terrible pain*) All my research has led to
contradictory revelations. I am left with nothing but
doubt. Terrible doubt. The painter spent his days
producing nothing but strokes of lead. His model
stopped attending to the dying. And there is no
shortage of them these days.

I have failed miserably. This morning, I allowed them
to dig a common grave. I give my sermons on the
church steps. Never in the history of the Church in
America have we closed the doors of our churches.
(*MARY ANNE takes off her blouse and, bare-breasted, she
hands him the whip.*) What are you doing?

MARY ANNE

It's my turn to expiate, Father.

YOUNG PRIEST

(*ill at ease*) Put your clothes back on, please.

MARY ANNE

Turn back into a slimy fish, with the head of a dog, the wings of a bird and the legs of a reptile covered in scales. A barque with larvae as oarsmen. (*She plunges her face between the YOUNG PRIEST's legs.*) Scare me, Father, scare me. I am yours.

YOUNG PRIEST

(*clearly disturbed*) Mary Anne, you are confusing your feelings for God with those inspired by his representative on Earth.

MARY ANNE

This will be my sacrifice. I want to expiate, to ward off the flu, to put an end to the war.

YOUNG PRIEST

What do you want from me? Do you want my trembling voice to betray my weakness? (*losing control, vehemently*) Get out of here! Get out!

MARY ANNE exits, ashamed. The YOUNG PRIEST falls on his knees. He crosses himself. Beat. The DOCTOR enters carrying a small black satchel.

YOUNG PRIEST

What are you doing here?

The DOCTOR opens his satchel and takes out a syringe and a vial of morphine.

DOCTOR

I heard your cries. (*The DOCTOR stares at the YOUNG PRIEST's bloody wounds.*)

You have to admit that she's talented.

YOUNG PRIEST

Just when my congregation needs me to guide them, when I should show true strength, everything collapses. I placed all my hopes in a grand scheme that only pleased my vanity. I placed all my confidence in an Italian who spends his days upsetting a troubled girl who confuses reality and myth, who confuses a manure-scorched field where nothing grows with a "field of secrets." I all but forced her to give herself to him. I allowed myself to be seduced by a silly girl who was the victim of a bad joke on the bank of the stream. And my own madness went so far, last night I decided to have my fortune read in my bed sheets.

DOCTOR
I have just what you need.

YOUNG PRIEST
(*shouting at him*) And now I am confiding in a man who is more like a butcher than a doctor. A man who never takes his eyes off my face.

DOCTOR
A taste of paradise and tomorrow you'll feel stronger.

YOUNG PRIEST
I don't even know if Jesus was beardless or not! (*He falls on his knees, in tears, and extends his arm.*) Yes ... Please!

DOCTOR
Morphine.

YOUNG PRIEST
Yes. A taste of paradise.

DOCTOR
(*injecting the shot of morphine*) Cheers, Father.

YOUNG PRIEST
Cheers!

DOCTOR
You'll see, it's very quick.

YOUNG PRIEST
Yes. A bit of quick paradise.

*Under the influence of the morphine, the YOUNG PRIEST
lies down on a table. The DOCTOR takes a shining
scalpel out of his satchel.*

DOCTOR
See how quickly the forehead relaxes. And the
wrinkles fade. Spread your wings, Father. Fly away!

YOUNG PRIEST
Sweet as the wine of Cana.

DOCTOR
Don't resist.

YOUNG PRIEST
Abundant as the great draught of fishes.

DOCTOR
Yes, you are in my net now. (*letting his scalpel graze the
YOUNG PRIEST's face*) From the Adam's apple. No.
From the chin. A straight thin line, precise. From the
lips, along the furrow beneath the nose, along the
centre of the nose to the hairline. I'll fold back the
edges of the skin, delicately. A thin layer of white fat.
I'll slip my fingers between the epidermis and the
fascia. The occipital muscle. The temporal. The
frontal. A faint mist will rise from the trachea. The
ephemeral cloud of life? The soul, perhaps? Perhaps
I will finally discover it? (*Beat.*) Time to double the
dose and begin.

TABLEAU 12

*MARY OF THE SECRETS enters holding a bouquet of wild
daisies.*

MARY OF THE SECRETS
(*in high spirits*) I've brought you some daisies,
Alessandro. They're not lilies, but we can pretend
they are. They grow in the field of secrets now, where
nothing grew before. How is the fresco coming
along, Alessandro? I love to repeat your name,
Alessandro. You seem so tired. You work too hard,
Alessandro. I love talking to you like this. Are you
hungry, Alessandro? Did you sleep well, Alessandro?
Tell me your dreams, Alessandro. Don't come home
too late, stay at my side, Alessandro! Alessandro!
Alessandro! I opened all the windows at my father's
house. Ours is the only house with the windows wide
open. The breeze is cool. We're the only ones who
get such a cool breeze. (*She caresses her belly.*) It will be
a son. I know. I can feel it. I've already started to talk
to him about you. We'll have to leave this village
soon. We will travel around and you will paint the
walls of all the churches. I'll pose for you, holding
our child at my breast. Say something, Alessandro.
(*Beat. He unwraps the painting slowly and shows it to her.
MARY OF THE SECRETS cannot believe her eyes.*) My face
looks so strange. Those aren't my eyes. That's not my
nose, or my mouth. It's nothing like me! You took all
this time to paint me so different? You gave me a

smile, but it's not my smile. You made me look
luminous, but it's not my light.

PAINTER
I was asked to paint a virgin.

MARY OF THE SECRETS
That's not me.

PAINTER
No. I just told you, I was asked to paint a virgin.
(*Long silence. MARY OF THE SECRETS drops the daisies.*) Se
ti stordissi di promesse che non manterrei? Se
diventassi la tua croce?

MARY OF THE SECRETS
I don't understand.

PAINTER
Hai ceduto ad ogni frase. I tuoi occhi hanno perduto
il loro dolore. Le labbra sono diventate banali.

MARY OF THE SECRETS
I don't understand your words.

PAINTER
Le mani monotone. Non fai che sognare la banalità
della felicitè coniugale. Ti volevo madonna bella,
bella e cupa. Non ho avuto che l'ennesima fidanzata.

*The PAINTER exits. MARY OF THE SECRETS falls on her
knees. We hear the murmuring of buried souls.*

MARY OF THE SECRETS
(*calmly*) Leave my body, embryo of hope. Leave my
body. Find two dead branches. Lift my skirts and knit
better than my mother.

Bells ring joyfully, announcing the Armistice.

Epilogue

The bells are ringing. The YOUNG PRIEST is kneeling in the church. His face is completely wrapped in bandages. Throughout this scene, he will appear to be transported in a flight of mystical ecstasy. MARY ANNE comes to join him.

MARY ANNE

It's Mary Anne, Father. You have succeeded. The flu is no longer killing anyone, the war is over, the painter has finished the fresco. You succeeded. (*touching his face*) They say you forgave the doctor. Blind and faceless, you have forgiven the doctor. You are a saint, Father. (*She kneels down beside the YOUNG PRIEST. She places her hands on his face.*) Your face will never take on another shape. A vegetable with eyes, a fish with the head of a dog, a barque of larvae, a scabby wound, a talking snake, a … priest. No. No shape at all. (*She kisses his hands.*) You are a saint, Father. Tell me what you see. Scare me, Father!

YOUNG PRIEST

We must close the doors to the church.

MARY ANNE

I'll help you, Father.

YOUNG PRIEST

Push harder!

MARY ANNE
The doors won't budge!

YOUNG PRIEST
(*Suddenly, as if stunned by what he "sees."*) Look at what's coming down the street.

MARY ANNE
I can't see a thing.

YOUNG PRIEST
A dark mass coming this way.

MARY ANNE
I don't want to see it. (*She closes her eyes and will keep them closed until the end of the scene.*)

YOUNG PRIEST
Heading right for us. A black bride carrying a deformed cherub in her arms. And leaving a long red trail behind her.

MARY ANNE
We have to close the doors, fast!

YOUNG PRIEST
A procession of ghosts precedes her. Can you hear it?

MARY ANNE
The wailing wind?

YOUNG PRIEST
No, those are the demons from the field of secrets. And listen to the thunder!

MARY ANNE
Thunder, at last!

YOUNG PRIEST
She is spitting and cursing us.

MARY ANNE
Yes, she is cursing us.

YOUNG PRIEST
> She is climbing the stairs of the church. The flame in the sanctuary is wavering.

MARY ANNE
> (*frightened but ecstatic*) Go on, Father.

YOUNG PRIEST
> More thunder.

MARY ANNE
> Yes, more thunder.

YOUNG PRIEST
> Look at her, she is opening her arms.

MARY ANNE
> She is staring at us.

YOUNG PRIEST
> Silently, she implores us to let her enter.

MARY ANNE
> Now she is going to enter the temple.

YOUNG PRIEST
> Yes.

MARY ANNE
> Now she is entering the temple.

YOUNG PRIEST
> Yes.

MARY ANNE
> She has entered the temple.

YOUNG PRIEST
> She is walking down the centre aisle. In her wake, Rome topples, Constantinople bows down, Babylon is kneeling. Humanity falls silent.

MARY ANNE
    (*whispering*) I heard humanity fall silent. You are
    extraordinary, Father.

YOUNG PRIEST
    A gust of wind bursts into the temple. It lifts her up.
    She enters the fresco. She enters the fresco and she
    rises. She rises to the heavens. It is the Ascension.
    (*He collapses, exhausted.*)

MARY ANNE
    Such inspiration, Father! I'm still trembling.

YOUNG PRIEST
    That is how I will tell the story to my congregation.

MARY ANNE
    I hope they'll be as frightened as I am.

YOUNG PRIEST
    Describe the fresco to me, Mary Anne. Be inspired.

    MARY ANNE opens her eyes.

MARY ANNE
    It's a triptych. On the left, there is a woman with her
    eyes closed and a devil with a dog's head peering
    through her legs. Another woman stands with her
    arms stretched out in longing, and her lips are
    stained with blood. On the right, a woman is
    suffocating in a sheet. The central panel depicts a
    Madonna on a cloud floating on a gust of coughs.
    Above her, a deformed cherub, and stars that failed
    to keep their promise. She is wearing a long veil torn
    in anger and belted by a whip. In her left hand, she
    is holding some wilted daisies, and with the right, she
    is cursing humanity. On her breast, her Sacred Heart
    is trapped in an iron crown, pierced by the sword of
    betrayal.

YOUNG PRIEST
    And her face? Describe her face.

Beat.

MARY ANNE
    It's yours, Father. It's your face.

YOUNG PRIEST
    Invent something better.

MARY ANNE
    No, Father. It's your face.

The End